~~MERCILESS~~ ~~SAVAGES~~ (not)

A how-to guide to help you write and talk respectfully about American Indians

Phil Bellfy

Ziibi Press

ISBN-13 979-8-89656-078-4 paperback
ISBN-13 979-8-89656-079-1 hardcover
ISBN-13 979-8-89656-080-7 eBook

Ziibi Press is an imprint of
Modern History Press
5145 Pontiac Trail
Ann Arbor, MI

More information at BeautifulLeaf.com

info@ModernHistoryPress.com
www.ModernHistoryPress.com

Tollfree 888-761-6268
FAX 734-663-6861
Distributed by Ingram (USA, CAN, AU, EU)

Cover art conjured up by the author and perpetrated by Jim Middleton, pharmacist, artist, and animator extraordinaire.

More on Jim's art can be found at:
https://www.animatingapothecary.blogspot.com

Contents

Declaration of Independence In Congress, July 4, 1776 1

Introduction 2

A Lexicon of Regrettable Terms 5

Apple 5

BIPOC –Black, Indigenous, People of Color.6

Blood Quantum..7

Brave; Buck; Chief.......................................8

Eskimo 9

Geronimo 10

Half Breed 11

Hold Down The Fort...................................12

Indian..13

Indian Giver 14

Injuns, ...15

Kickapoo ("Joy Juice")..............................16

Military Terminology (USA) 17

Moccasins (Walk A Mile In Their 20

Niggers 21

Off the Reservation.................................... 22

Papoose 23

Pocahontas/Squaw 24

Posse... 25

Powwow.. 26

Race 27

Red Tape – White Tape 28

Redskins 29

Savage 30

Savagism... 31

Scalping 32

Smoke Signals 33

Squaw... 34

Taming of the West 35

Thanksgiving 36

Tonto.. 37

Too Many Chiefs – Not Enough Indians .. 38

Totem Pole (Low Man On The) 39

Tribe/Tribal... 40

Circle the Wagons 41

Wagon-Burners 42

iv

Wahoo..43

War Paint / Warpath 44

Yahoo..45

Tonto's Last Stand 46

Appendix: "Body Ritual Among The Nacirema" By Horace Miner 47

About the Author 61

Declaration of Independence In Congress, July 4, 1776

The unanimous Declaration of the thirteen united States of America states:

When in the Course of human events, it becomes necessary for one people to dissolve the political bands which have connected them with another, and to assume among the powers of the earth, the separate and equal station to which the Laws of Nature and of Nature's God entitle them, a decent respect to the opinions of mankind requires that they should declare the causes which impel them to the separation... He has excited domestic insurrections amongst us, and has endeavoured to bring on the inhabitants of our frontiers, **the merciless Indian Savages,** whose known rule of warfare, is an undistinguished destruction of all ages, sexes and conditions...."

Introduction

As the US Declaration, presented above, refers to the Native people of this continent as "merciless savages," it's all but impossible to counter such misguided rhetoric, but this book will try to do just that.

First is the obvious: "savages" should never be used to refer to any indigenous peoples, North American, or otherwise. It is horrible, false, and obviously demeaning.

Secondarily, the same might be said about "Indians" generally. Personally, I don't think that you should avoid the term at all times. For example, if you are making a historical reference (like pointing to the "Indian Civilization Act" of 1819) use of the term Indian is not only appropriate it is required to insure historical accuracy.

At the same time, use of the term American Indian will not raise many critical eyebrows; nor will the use of Aboriginal People (the Canadian Constitutional choice), but, at the same time, you should avoid "Aborigines" as a general term, as this is an Australian "legal term" for the continent's indigenous people.

So, in that context, Indigenous People, used as a general collective term, is also an acceptable term for the people "indigenous" to this hemisphere.

But, if you need to refer to "indigenous" people, I would suggest using the specific reference to the specific people you are referring to. For example: I am a Member of the White Earth Band of Minnesota Chippewa. And as Gerald Vizenor has pointed out. "Chippewa" is a term that is used in US treaties to refer to us; therefore, in that context, use of Chippewa is "the law." But, you should also be aware that in that exact context (treaty "law"), Ojibway is used in the British/Canadian context.

With that in mind, I suggest that you use the term that the peoples that you are referring to, use the term that they use. In the Chippewa/Ojibway context referenced above, we refer to ourselves as the Anishinaabeg (the plural; one of us is an Anishinaabe).

I don't have the time or the space to point out to you the specific "collective' term used by the hundreds of Tribal people in the hemisphere. But if you are serious about writing about (or speaking about) a group of Indigenous people, take the time and expend the effort to use the term they use to refer to themselves.

My own book, *Indians and Other Misnomers: A Cross-Reference Dictionary of the People, Persons, and Places of Native North America,* published by Fulcrum Press in 2001, would be an invaluable continent-wide resource.

My most recent book, published by Ziibi Press in 2023, *Indians and Other Misnomers of the Upper Great Lakes*, should also be very helpful if your reference is to Tribes and/or First Nations of the Upper Great Lakes. Finally I would suggest that you should be careful when using Internet sources, as I've seen quite a bit of suspect Tribal name "translations." If you have the option, I suggest using the oldest term available from a Tribal source, as it is most likely the one used by those closest to "contact" with Europeans.

Apple

When used to refer to a Native person, should be avoided. It's meaning is derogatory—red on the outside, white on the inside. "Radish" has also been used in the same context; avoid its use, too.

BIPOC –Black, Indigenous, People of Color.

This acronym simply displays a mental laziness. If you want to write about Black folk, just do it, or Indigenous folk, just do that. As for "people of color," again, it shows no respect to simply lump them all together into a "POC" acronym.

Blood Quantum

"How much 'Indian" are you"?

Any question along these lines, is deeply offensive and a question or a reference that should be avoided at all times (unless you're talking about kennel-club dogs).

The "official" term is "Degree of Indian Blood." To be honest, this DIB is part of what it means to be a Member of an Indian Tribe, or First Nation as these settler societies move to resolve their "Indian Problem" by adhering to a strictly racist "definition" of who is an "Indian," and who is not. As Indian people "inter-marry" with non-Indians, their DIB drops below "acceptable" levels and the "Indian" disappears.

The Bureau of Indian Affairs sets the "standard' of one-quarter or more of DIB to be an "Indian." Tribes and First Nations are "allowed" by the settler states to set their DIB at any level they wish. Some have decided to "classify" their members/citizens to be 100% indigenous.

Brave; Buck; Chief

Referring to a male American Indian as "chief" should be avoided; unless the referent is actually a person elected to that office. Chief would then be a title, and could be used to refer to any person elected to that high office.

A better usage would be to use the term for a "chief" of the Tribe you are referring to; in the language of the Ojibway/Chippewa, that word would be Ogema (plural; Ogemuk). A Google-search should help you find the appropriate word for your usage,

The same arguments can be used for Brave and Buck when referring to a male American Indian --demeaning in any context.

Eskimo

The name means something like "Eaters of Raw Meat," which has been perverted to imply that these people were cannibals. Use Inuit instead and avoid any controversy.

You also might be interested in the word the Inuit use for the "visitors" —Kabloona—Those Who Pamper Their Eyebrows (a reference to the settlers' apparent personal vanity).

Geronimo

US military "war cry," occasionally used by jumping paratroopers or, more generally, anyone about to jump from a great height, or as a general exclamation of exhilaration.

It's likely that the U.S. operation to kill Osama bin Laden used the code name "Geronimo" to refer to either the overall operation, to fugitive bin Laden himself, or to the act of killing or capturing bin Laden.

Half Breed

Used to refer to a person of "mixed blood" ancestry, usually that of a Native woman and a European.

A much better term would be Métis, which is a Constitutional designation in Canada comprising one of the recognized groups of "Aboriginal People."

This "half-breed" offensive term is often implied when an Indigenous person is asked: "what's your blood quantum?" Blood quantum (officially called Degree of Indian Blood [see above]) is a deeply offensive term, although mandated by "settler" governments which is universally used to determine who is an "Indian" as a requirement for services, or "membership" in many Tribes and First Nations. The entire concept of demanding a certain DIB for services is an attempt to eliminate the "Indian Problem" (and save lots of money) through racist eugenic "standards."

The counterpart to this genocidal madness is the now abandoned "one drop rule" to identify African Americans.

Hold Down The Fort

Has probably been around since before 1776, but it seems to imply that someone should "hold down the fort" against Indians attacking it. To avoid the confusing implication, try another characterization to refer to someone else "put in charge temporarily."

Indian

("Behaving like a wild," etc.) See the Introduction, above.

Aside from the obvious "misnomer" of the term (Columbus was nowhere near India when he "ran into" what is now referred to as The West Indies), use of "Indian" is often confused with the people of India.

I had a friend who, over a period of time, discussed Philosophy with a person from India. They came up with the designations "Feather Indians," and "Dot Indians" to avoid the problem of using "Indian" as a general designation.

American Indian will do in its stead.

Indian Giver

During the colonial period, settlers would often exchange gifts with Native people, as that was their custom. When British settlers refused to reciprocate with gifts of relative equal value, the Native people were greatly offended and often demanded their "gifts" be returned, giving rise to the term "Indian giver." Simply, the British couldn't understand the value of "gift-giving," preferring "trade" for money in its place.

I won't go into the entire history here, But the French/Indian "trading" regime operated on a much more equal series of gift-giving before the actual "trade" took place. The refusal of the British to follow this French/Native protocol eventually led to "Pontiac's Rebellion" (which I prefer to call "Pontiac's Vigorous Defense of the Homeland).

After the "Rebellion," the British decided it was prudent to follow the French "trading" protocol to some degree.

Injuns

To be avoided at all cost.

Consider this:

The Lone Ranger and Tonto headed to the saloon for some sarsaparilla after a hard day fighting evil.. The Lone Ranger's horse, Silver, was pretty hot and sweaty after their action and their trek, so the Lone Ranger had Tonto run around the horse, fanning it with his ten-gallon-hat.

A stranger in the bar came up to the Lone Ranger and asked him if that was his horse outside overheated. When the Lone Ranger said, yes, it was, the stranger said—well, it's no wonder; you left your injun running!

Kickapoo ("Joy Juice")

The Kickapoo were originally in the area south of the Great Lakes; they now reside in Kansas, Texas, and Oklahoma, the result of the 1830's Removal Policy.

"Kickapoo Joy Juice" is rather derogatory as it suggests that native people like their liquor of "stupefying potency, so strong that the fumes alone were known to melt the rivets off of battleships." (This from Al Capp, the author of the Li'l Abner comic strip).

Should be avoided in all cases so as to avoid any "drunken Indian" allusions.

Military Terminology (USA)

Also see Geronimo –

- AH-56 Cheyenne attack helicopter
- AH-64 Apache attack helicopter[5]
- ARH-70 Arapaho attack/recon helicopter
- BGM-109 Tomahawk cruise missile
- C-12 Huron transport aircraft[5]
- CH-37 Mohave heavy-lift helicopter
- CH-47 Chinook heavy-lift transport helicopter[5]
- CH-54 Tarhe heavy lift helicopter. Tarhe was a Wyandot ogema (chief).
- H-13 Sioux helicopter, the first one.
- H-21 Shawnee transport helicopter
- H-34 Choctaw transport helicopter[5]
- MH 6 Little Bird light helicopter. Ogimauh-binaessih; translates to Chief Little Bird, a Mississauga Ojibway Chief.
- OH-58 Kiowa observation helicopter[5]
- OH-6 Cayuse observation helicopter[5]
- OV-1 Mohawk twin-engine observation aircraft[5]

- RAH-66 Comanche recon/attack helicopter
- RU-8 Seminole utility aircraft[5]
- T-41 Mescalero trainer aircraft[5]
- TH-67 Creek trainer helicopter[5]
- U-21 Ute utility aircraft[5]
- UH-1 Iroquois utility helicopter[5]
- UH-60 Black Hawk utility helicopter[5]
- UH-72 Lakota utility helicopter
- USNS *Sacagawea*
- USS *Chickasaw*

If you find yourself in the position, for example, of referring to a "Tomahawk" missile, just use "cruise missile' instead. Ditch the Native designator; it's totally unnecessary.

"Indian Country" was often used to refer to Vietnam during that war. I'm sure you can readily discern how offensive that was. Don't make the same mistake.

Second Infantry Division Insignia-- USA

Moccasins (Walk A Mile In Their)

From a line in an 1895 poem, "Judge Softly," by Mary T. Lathrap.

No need to conjure up Indigenous people with this "poetic" reference; "Walk a Mile in His Shoes" will work just as well.

Niggers

Sand Niggers; Prairie Niggers; Timber Niggers.

Obviously offensive in any context (Sand Niggers referred to Indigenous People of the Southwest; Prairie Niggers referred to Indigenous People of the Great Plains; Timber Niggers referred to Indigenous People of the Upper Great Lakes). Never appropriate to be used except in an "Anti-Indian" historical context.

There are, sadly, too many regional variations to list here. Avoid them all.

Off the Reservation

This phrase refers to the aftermath of the "Indian Wars" of the West, where, after the bison were slaughtered, Native People were herded on to "reservations" where they had to depend on government "rations" to survive. Often these rations were withheld to further subjugate the Indians.

When this happened, which was often, the government declared that any Indians found to be "off the reservation"(hunting for increasingly scarce bison and other game) were "hostiles" and could—and should—be shot on sight.

Although currently widely used in a variety of contexts, the phrase should not be used at all, and there is no acceptable alternative that I can think of.

Papoose

A board with a pouch for carrying a Native American Baby; now used to refer to the child, itself (or any child). Considered by some to be derogatory, so it should be avoided—*baby* works just fine.

Pocahontas/Squaw

Donald Trump's continual reference to senator Elizabeth Warren as "Pocahontas" is totally unacceptable in any context, as is the "S-word." While it is true that local use of the S-word is beyond public control, it should be noted that both the US and Canadian governments have eliminated or changed that term in every place name that is subject to their jurisdiction.

The equivalent in English is the "C-word".

Both are deeply offensive and should never be used in any context.

Posse

Sometimes used to refer to a group of Native American warriors who would band together for hunting, protection, or raiding parties, essentially acting like a "war party." It's OK to use, but if there is any confusion with the use in the Native context, don't go there.

Powwow

The "pow-wow" in the Native context is the spiritual leader in the healing ceremonies which now, often, bear that same name. Unless it is used in that Native ceremonial context, you should use another term.

Also, just FYI, if there is a fee to attend a Powwow or any other Indigenous ceremony; you should be deeply suspicious of the intent of the organizers. Would you be comfortable if you were asked to pay to attend an "established" church service?

Race

Again, this is one my personal no-nos. I know it's common usage to refer to the "White race," the Black race," the Yellow race," and the "Red race, but I like to think there is only one "race," the "human race."

Use of these "different races" only serves to divide us into categories, making it easier to discriminate and control "the masses" through a "divide-and-conquer" mentality. Don't fall into that trap.

If you'd like a thorough examination of the concept of "race," I suggest that you read _The Mismeasure of Man_, by Stephen Jay Gould.

Your local library should have a copy.

Red Tape – White Tape

I have to be honest, this entry is purely personal. I know the true meaning and origin of "red tape," but in today's bureaucratic context, it's really "white tape" —excessive and/or unnecessary government regulations and bureaucratic delay promulgated by settler governments to impede actions by those confronting that frustrating-by-design "white tape."

Which brings to mind one of my favorite words: beadledom—a stupid or officious display or exercise of authority associated with petty officials who exercise that "authority" just because they can. That's what "red tape" often is.

Redskins

We should all be delighted by the decision of the Washington football team to "retire" that deeply offensive "mascot" term.

The term derives from the colonial practice of offering bounties for Native scalps, that is, a bounty for a "redskin."

It's entirely possible that the "taking of scalps" by Plains Tribes arose from that genocidal colonial practice.

If you nccd morc information and background, you should watch the documentary "In Whose Honor" about the use of Native imagery and names in the sports mascot controversy.

Savage

Dictionary meaning: extremely violent, wild, or frightening.

From the latin—silvaticus—meaning, in a state of nature, of a woodland. This Latin root became "salvages" in Spanish, "sauvage" in French.

The Inquisition held that those who lived in the woods, or "worshipped" there, were in league with the devil. That's partly how the word got its racist and derogatory meaning. It should never be used in any kind of "native" context.

Also, consider "heathen," which means nothing more than those who lived in the heath, that is, those who lived in open or uncultivated land.

Or pagans, from the Latin "paganus"; a villager, a rustic. Lastly, consider the original meaning of barbarian: one whose culture and language differs from my own.

If you use of any of these words, you should be aware of their roots and be mindful of how these descriptors of human beings came to be wholly derogatory.

Savagism

According to this more-or-less formal "philosophy, "Indians" are (1) emotional rather than rational, (2) morally and culturally deficient, (3) uncivilized, (4) genetically inferior, (5) untrustworthy (although individuals have the potential to be "noble"), (6) generally lazy and indolent, and (7) often immorally sensual in their nature. More reason to avoid "savage" and similar terms.

Scalping

Any reference to scalps in any context should be avoided; like political fights devolving into the taking of "scalps."

Also, see Redskins, above.

Smoke Signals

Again, I see no need to bring up Native imagery when referring to the sending of messages over long distances (we now have the Internet for that).

Squaw

See *Pocahontas*, above.

Must be avoided in every case.

Often used in place names, businesses, etc., the "S-word" is just one of hundreds of place names using native-derived words of questionable value. Whenever tempted to use, one, be sure that the context is not derogatory or controversial.

Taming of the West

The "taming" of the West refers to the elimination of the "free Indian: who "roamed" the vast territory west of the Mississippi through a series of "wars" waged on the true occupants and "owners" of this vast territory.

The phrase has only one meaning—the "taming of the West" could only be accomplished by killing of the Indians, often taking the form of massacres of innocents.

See also "off the reservation" in this volume.

Thanksgiving

Thanksgiving is a modern holiday that started in colonial New England, specifically, when a day of thanksgiving was declared for God giving the settlers a "glorious victory": after their massacre of the Pequot village near what is now Mystic, Connecticut, in 1637. The "tradition" of declaring a Day of Thanksgiving after each slaughter of Indians became commonplace throughout colonial New England.

I'm not suggesting that no one should celebrate "Thanksgiving," just that when you do, you reflect on the true origins of that holiday. And, of course, Thanksgiving meals consist of food indigenous to the colonies; gifts from the Native people who's slaughter is being "celebrated."

When the Pilgrims landed on Plymouth Rock, some of us thought it should have been the other way around.

Tonto

Considered by most to be a term of derision, and wholly unacceptable in reference to an American Indian.

As the "sidekick" of the Lone Ranger, Tonto was often portrayed as an ignorant fool (the Spanish definition of the word).

See "Injuns" and "Yahoo" entries in this volume.

Too Many Chiefs – Not Enough Indians

Sometimes used to describe a situation where there are too many people giving orders and not enough people to carry them out.

How this terminology came to be accepted parlance is beyond me.

Totem Pole (Low Man On The)

Offensive idiom that has no cultural or historical relevance.

The word totem refers to a guardian or ancestral being, usually supernatural, that is revered and respected. The significance of the real or mythological animal carved on a totem pole is its identification with the lineage of the head of the household. More widely known, but in fact far less common, are the elaborately carved tall totem poles that relate an entire family legend in the form of a "totem pole."

Only with an understanding of what the symbols mean to the Native Americans and knowledge of the history and customs of the clan involved can the pole be interpreted. Each animal or spirit carved on the pole has meaning, and when combined on the pole in sequence, each figure is an important symbolic constituent of a story or myth.

Tribe/Tribal

Use of the term in the positive sense would be: characteristic of a tribe, a social group with a shared culture language and customs. This usage is not offensive, but in general colloquial use, the terms have come to imply a blind loyalty or a narrow-minded perspective. I suggest that either word should not be used so as to never bring up the negative connotations associated with "tribe" and/or "tribal."

Use of Tribe is perfectly ok when used as a formal descriptor, as in "Apache Tribe." In this context, I suggest using the capital "T."

Circle the Wagons

My very least favorite "pet peeve" phrase, very widely used without any knowledge or awareness of its source—the so-called "Taming of the West" (also in this volume).

It is clearly culturally insensitive and evokes racist images of Native Americans and its use should always be avoided.

I find the Wikipedia article on the *Treaty of Fort Laramie* to be a fairly accurate summary of the tremendous problems faced by Native Americans due to the "Manifest Destiny" invasion of their Great Plains homelands, and the accompanying decimation of the bison herds which supplied the Plains Indians with their sustenance. It is true that the Native people may have attacked the settlers' wagon trains that invaded and threatened their very existence, but that does not justify the use of this, and related, terms.

It should be noted that this treaty is the only one in the history of the US that was signed by the US wherein the provisions were dictated by "winning party"—the Plains Indians—to court cases and controversy to this day.

https://en.wikipedia.org/wiki/Treaty_of_Fort_Lar amie_(1868).

Wagon-Burners

Wagon Burners and similar terms used in this "Taming of the West" context should never be used—they simply reinforce the "merciless savage" imagery found in the US Declaration of Independence, and, sadly, in countless other contexts.

Wahoo

A term of opprobrium, and, therefore, should always be avoided.

The "Chief Wahoo" mascot for the Cleveland baseball team was abandoned in 2019, due to its demeaning stereotypical usage and meaning.

See, Yahoo, below.

War Paint / Warpath

Used to refer to the assumed savage nature of American Indians.

Use a different term that doesn't include a reference to Native people (not sure what a non-Native equivalent would be, to be honest). And don't ever don "warpaint" as a cosmetic augmentation—"make-up" works just as well).

Yahoo

There is controversy over the possible "Native" person source, but the term is most often used to refer to "a loud, rude, uneducated, or boorish person." To avoid the controversy, avoid its use.

The Lone Ranger's Last Stand

The Lone Ranger and Tonto were riding through a valley on their way to their camp after a hard day of fighting evil outlaws. At one point in the canyon, the Lone Ranger looked up and saw the ridge to the right was filled with Apache warriors; the ridge to the left was also filled with warriors; the same for behind them, and in front of them. They were surrounded! The Lone Ranger turned to Tonto and said—"It looks like we've come to the end of our trail." Tonto replied— "What you mean 'we,' paleface?"

Appendix:
"Body Ritual Among The Nacirema"
By Horace Miner

The anthropologist has become so familiar with the diversity of ways in which different people behave in similar situations that he is not apt to be surprised by even the most exotic customs. In fact, if all of the logically possible combinations of behavior have not been found somewhere in the world, he is apt to suspect that they must be present in some yet undescribed tribe. The point has, in fact, been expressed with respect to clan organization by Murdock[1]. In this light, the magical beliefs and practices of the Nacirema present such unusual aspects that it seems desirable to describe them as an example of the extremes to which human behavior can go.

Professor Linton[2] first brought the ritual of the Nacirema to the attention of anthropologists ninety years ago, but the culture of this people is still very poorly understood. They are a North American group living in the territory between the Canadian Cree, the Yaqui and Tarahumare of Mexico, and the Carib and Arawak of the Antilles. Little is known of their origin, although tradition states that they came from the east. According to Nacirema mythology, their nation was originated by a culture hero, Notgnihsaw, who is otherwise known for two great feats of strength—the throwing of a piece of wampum across the river Pa-To-Mac and the chopping down of a cherry tree in which the Spirit of Truth resided.

Nacirema culture is characterized by a highly developed market economy which has evolved in a rich natural habitat. While much of the people's time is devoted to economic pursuits, a large part of the fruits of these labors and a considerable portion of the day are spent in ritual activity. The focus of this activity is the human body, the appearance and health of which loom as a dominant concern in the ethos of the people. While such a concern is certainly not unusual, its ceremonial aspects and associated philosophy are unique.

The fundamental belief underlying the whole

system appears to be that the human body is ugly and that its natural tendency is to debility and disease. Incarcerated in such a body, man's only hope is to avert these characteristics through the use of ritual and ceremony. Every household has one or more shrines devoted to this purpose. The more powerful individuals in the society have several shrines in their houses and, in fact, the opulence of a house is often referred to in terms of the number of such ritual centers it possesses. Most houses are of wattle and daub construction, but the shrine rooms of the more wealthy are walled with stone. Poorer families imitate the rich by applying pottery plaques to their shrine walls.

While each family has at least one such shrine, the rituals associated with it are not family ceremonies but are private and secret. The rites are normally only discussed with children, and then only during the period when they are being initiated into these mysteries. I was able, how-ever, to establish sufficient rapport with the natives to examine these shrines and to have the rituals described to me.

The focal point of the shrine is a box or chest which is built into the wall. In this chest are kept the many charms and magical potions without which no native believes he could live. These preparations are secured from a variety of specialized practitioners. The most powerful of these are the medicine men, whose assistance must be rewarded with substantial gifts. However, the medicine men do not provide the curative potions for their clients, but decide what the ingredients should be and then write them down in an ancient and secret language. This writing is understood only by the medicine men and by the herbalists who, for another gift, provide the required charm.

The charm is not disposed of after it has served its purpose, but is placed in the charmbox of the household shrine. As these magical materials are specific for certain ills, and the real or imagined maladies of the people are many, the charm-box is usually full to overflowing. The magical packets are so numerous that people forget what their purposes were and fear to use them again. While the natives are very vague on this point, we can only assume that the idea in retaining all the old magical materials is that their presence in the charm-box, before which the body rituals are conducted, will in some way protect the worshiper.

Beneath the charm-box is a small font. Each day every member of the family, in succession, enters the shrine room, bows his head before the charm-box, mingles different sorts of holy water in the font, and proceeds with a brief rite of ablution[3]. The holy waters are secured from the Water Temple of the community, where the priests conduct elaborate ceremonies to make the liquid ritually pure.

In the hierarchy of magical practitioners, and below the medicine men in prestige, are specialists whose designation is best translated as "holy-mouth-men." The Nacirema have an almost pathological horror of and fascination with the mouth, the condition of which is believed to have a supernatural influence on all social relationships. Were it not for the rituals of the mouth, they believe that their teeth would fall out, their gums bleed, their jaws shrink, their friends desert them, and their lovers reject them. They also believe that a strong relationship exists between oral and moral characteristics. For example, there is a ritual ablution of the mouth for children which is supposed to improve their moral fiber.

The daily body ritual performed by everyone includes a mouth-rite. Despite the fact that these people are so punctilious [4] about care of the mouth, this rite involves a practice which strikes the uninitiated stranger as revolting. It was reported to me that the ritual consists of inserting a small bundle of hog hairs into the mouth, along with certain magical powders, and then moving the bundle in a highly formalized series of gestures.[5]

In addition to the private mouth-rite, the people seek out a holy-mouth-man once or twice a year. These practitioners have an impressive set of paraphernalia, consisting of a variety of augers, awls, probes, and prods. The use of these items in the exorcism of the evils of the mouth involves almost unbelievable ritual torture of the client. The holy-mouth-man opens the client's mouth and, using the above mentioned tools, enlarges any holes which decay may have created in the teeth. Magical materials are put into these holes. If there are no naturally occurring holes in the teeth, large sections of one or more teeth are gouged out so that the supernatural substance can be applied. In the client's view, the purpose of these ministrations[6] is to arrest decay and to draw friends. The extremely sacred and traditional character of the rite is evident in the fact that the natives return to the holy-mouth-men year after year, despite the fact that their teeth continue to decay.

It is to be hoped that, when a thorough study of the Nacirema is made, there will be careful inquiry into the personality structure of these people. One has but to watch the gleam in the eye of a holy-mouth-man, as he jabs an awl into an exposed nerve, to suspect that a certain amount of sadism is involved. If this can be established, a very interesting pattern emerges, for most of the population shows definite masochistic tendencies. It was to these that Professor Linton referred in discussing a distinctive part of the daily body ritual which is performed only by men. This part of the rite includes scraping and lacerating the surface of the face with a sharp instrument. Special women's rites are performed only four times during each lunar month, but what they lack in frequency is made up in barbarity. As part of this ceremony, women bake their heads in small ovens for about an hour. The theoretically interesting point is that what seems to be a preponderantly masochistic people have devel-oped sadistic specialists.

The medicine men have an imposing temple, or *latipso*, in every community of any size.

The more elaborate ceremonies required to treat very sick patients can only be performed at this temple. These ceremonies involve not only the thaumaturge[7] but a permanent group of vestal maidens who move sedately about the temple chambers in distinctive costume and headdress.

The *latipso* ceremonies are so harsh that it is phenomenal that a fair proportion of the really sick natives who enter the temple ever recover. Small children whose indoctrination is still incomplete have been known to resist attempts to take them to the temple because "that is where you go to die." Despite this fact, sick adults are not only willing but eager to undergo the protracted ritual purification, if they can afford to do so. No matter how ill the supplicant or how grave the emergency, the guardians of many temples will not admit a client if he cannot give a rich gift to the custodian. Even after one has gained and survived the ceremonies, the guardians will not permit the neophyte to leave until he makes still another gift.

The supplicant entering the temple is first stripped of all his or her clothes. In everyday life the Nacirema avoids exposure of his body and its natural functions. Bathing and excretory acts are performed only in the secrecy of the household shrine, where they are ritualized as part of the body-rites. Psychological shock results from the fact that body secrecy is suddenly lost upon entry into the *latipso*. A man, whose own wife has never seen him in an excretory act, suddenly finds himself naked and assisted by a vestal maiden while he performs his natural functions into a sacred vessel. This sort of ceremonial treatment is necessitated by the fact that the excreta are used by a diviner to ascertain the course and nature of the client's sickness. Female clients, on the other hand, find their naked bodies are subjected to the scrutiny, man-ipulation and prodding of the medicine men.

Few supplicants in the temple are well enough to do anything but lie on their hard beds. The daily ceremonies, like the rites of the holy-mouth-men, involve discomfort and torture. With ritual precision, the vestals awaken their miserable charges each dawn and roll them about on their beds of pain while performing ablutions, in the formal movements of which the maidens are highly trained. At other times they insert magic wands in the supplicant's mouth or force him to eat substances which are supposed to be healing. From time to time the medicine men come to their clients and jab magically treated needles into their flesh. The fact that these temple ceremonies may not cure, and may even kill the neophyte, in no way decreases the people's faith in the medicine men.

There remains one other kind of practitioner, known as a "listener." This witchdoctor has the power to exorcise the devils that lodge in the heads of people who have been bewitched. The Nacirema believe that parents bewitch their own children. Mothers are particularly suspected of putting a curse on children while teaching them the secret body rituals. The counter-magic of the witchdoctor is unusual in its lack of ritual. The patient simply tells the "listener" all his troubles and fears, beginning with the earliest difficulties he can remember. The memory displayed by the Nacirema in these exorcism sessions is truly remarkable. It is not uncommon for the patient to bemoan the rejection he felt upon being weaned as a babe, and a few individuals even see their troubles going back to the traumatic effects of their own birth.

In conclusion, mention must be made of certain practices which have their base in native esthetics but which depend upon the pervasive aversion to the natural body and its functions. There are ritual fasts to make fat people thin and ceremonial feasts to make thin people fat. Still other rites are used to make women's breasts larger if they are small, and smaller if they are large. General dissatisfaction with breast shape is symbolized in the fact that the ideal form is virtually outside the range of human variation. A few women afflicted with almost inhuman hyper-mammary development are so idolized that they make a handsome living by simply going from village to village and permitting the natives to stare at them for a fee.

Reference has already been made to the fact that excretory functions are ritualized, routinized, and relegated to secrecy. Natural reproductive functions are similarly distorted. Intercourse is taboo as a topic and scheduled as an act. Efforts are made to avoid pregnancy by the use of magical materials or by limiting intercourse to certain phases of the moon. Conception is actually very infrequent. When pregnant, women dress so as to hide their condition. Parturition takes place in secret, without friends or relatives to assist, and the majority of women do not nurse their infants.

Our review of the ritual life of the Nacirema has certainly shown them to be a magic-ridden people. It is hard to understand how they have managed to exist so long under the burdens which they have imposed upon themselves. But even such exotic customs as these take on real meaning when they are viewed with the insight provided by Malinowski[8] when he wrote:

Looking from far and above, from our high places of safety in the developed civilization, it is easy to see all the crudity and irrelevance of magic. But without its power and guidance early man could not have mastered his practical difficulties as he has done, nor could man have advanced to the higher stages of civilization.

Footnotes

1. Murdock, George P. 1949. *Social Structure*. NY: The Macmillan Co., page 71. George Peter Murdock (1897-1996 [?]) is a famous ethnographer. ↵

2. Linton, Ralph. 1936. *The Study of Man*. NY: D. Appleton-Century Co. page 326. Ralph Linton (1893-1953) is best known for studies of enculturation (maintaining that all culture is learned rather than inherited; the process by which a society's

culture is transmitted from one generation to the next), claiming culture is humanity's "social heredity."

3. A washing or cleansing of the body or a part of the body. From the Latin *abluere*, to wash away

4. Marked by precise observance of the finer points of etiquette and formal conduct.

5. It is worthy of note that since Prof. Miner's original research was conducted, the Nacirema have almost universally abandoned the natural bristles of their private mouth-rite in favor of oil-based polymerized synthetics. Additionally, the powders associated with this ritual have generally been semi-liquefied. Other updates to the Nacirema culture shall be eschewed in this document for the sake of parsimony.

6. Tending to religious or other important functions

7. A miracle-worker.

8. Malinowski, Bronislaw. *Magic, Science, and Religion*. Glencoe: The Free Press, page 70. Bronislaw Malinowski (1884-1942) is a famous cultural anthropologist best known for his argument that people everywhere

share common biological and psychological needs and that the function of all cultural institutions is to fulfill such needs; the nature of the institution is determined by its function.

An elder once remarked that the Americans were a truly backward people.

The average American Indian family consists of a mother, a father, several children, some aunties and uncles, perhaps a grandmother and/or a grandfather, and/or cousins, several dogs, and an anthropologist.

https://courses.lumenlearning.com/readinganthology/chapter/body-ritual-among-the-nacirema-by-horace-miner/

About the Author

Dr. Phil Bellfy is an enrolled member of the White Earth Band of Minnesota Chippewa. He now resides in the Ceded Territory now-known as the Upper Peninsula of Michigan at a place called Bawating (Sault Ste. Marie), within sight of the Medicine Line that separates the US and Canada.

Phil is a Co-founder of the Center for the Study of Indigenous Border Issues (CSIBI), and Editor and Publisher of its "education arm": the Ziibi Press.

He is Professor Emeritus of American Indian Studies, Michigan State University.

Dr. Bellfy is an, artist, an activist, and an award-winning author.

Learn more at BeautifulLeaf.com

No less than 27 out of the 50 states' names in the USA are based in American Indian languages. Additionally, six out of 13 of Canada's provinces and territories have names with indigenous origins, and, of course, Canada itself is derived from an indigenous source.

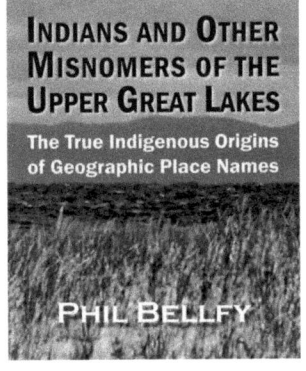

INDIANS AND OTHER MISNOMERS OF THE UPPER GREAT LAKES

The True Indigenous Origins of Geographic Place Names

PHIL BELLFY

Shakespeare quipped, "What's in a name?" A lot, it turns out, because states like California and Florida reflect their Spanish history; here, in the Great Lakes, that history is indigenous. If you have an understanding of the name of a place, its history may reveal itself. And that history will, most likely, enrich your own life and your place in it.

Join us on this journey seven Midwest states and Ontario as we alphabetically traverse indigenous place names in each locale. Alternately, you can peruse an alphabetical concordance of every place name. In the appendices, you'll discover details of US and Canadian treaties with indigenous people, and many that are still under dispute today-- including the Anishinaabek, Ottawa, Chippewa, Potawatomi, Miami, Kickapoo, Sauk, Sioux, Ojibway, Mississauga, Mohawk, Algonquin, Iroquois, Huron, and First Nations bands

ISBN 978-1-61599-742-8 * From Ziibi Press

The Great Lakes Basin is under severe ecological threat from fracking, bursting pipelines, sulfide mining, abandonment of government environmental regulation, invasive species, warming and lowering of the lakes, etc. This book presents essays on Traditional Knowledge, Indigenous Responsibility, and how Indigenous people, governments, and NGOs are responding to the environmental degradation which threatens the Great Lakes. This volume grew out of a conference that was held on the campus of Michigan State University on Earth Day, 2007.

All of the essays have been updated and revised for this book. Among the presenters were Ward Churchill (author and activist), Joyce Tekahnawiiaks King (Director, Akwesasne Justice Department), Frank Ettawageshik, (Executive Director of the United Tribes of Michigan), Aaron Payment (Chair of the Sault Sainte Marie Tribe of Chippewa Indians), and Dean Sayers (Chief of the Batchewana First Nation). Winona LaDuke (author, activist, twice Green Party VP candidate) also contributed to this volume.

978-1-61599-625-4

From Ziibi Press

BeautifulLeaf.com

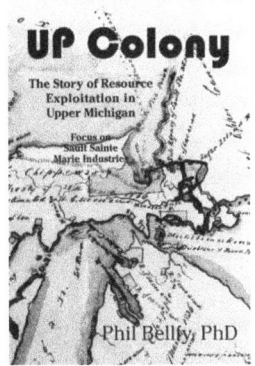

UP Colony

The Story of Resource Exploitation in Upper Michigan

Focus on Sault Sainte Marie Industries

Phil Bellfy, PhD

In the 1980s, Phil Bellfy pondered the question: Why does Sault, Ontario, appear to be so prosperous, while the "Sault" on the American side has fallen into such a deplorable state? Could the answer be that the "American side" was little more than a "resource colony"-or to use the academic jargon of "Conflict and Change" Sociology-an "Internal Colony." In UP Colony, Bellfy revisits his graduate research to update us the state of the Sault.

The ultimate question: why has the U.P.'s vast wealth, nearly unrivaled in the whole of the United States, left the area with poverty nearly unrivaled in the whole of the United States? None of the conventional explanations from "distance to markets," to "too many people," to "disadvantageous production costs," have any credibility. Simply put: "Where did the $1.5 billion earned from copper mining, $1 billion from logging, and nearly $4 billion in iron ore go?"

ISBN 97-8-1-61599-606-3

From Ziibi Press

BeautifulLeaf.com